CHILDREN'S ART

CHILDREN'S ART

A STUDY OF NORMAL DEVELOPMENT IN
CHILDREN'S MODES OF VISUALIZATION

BY MIRIAM LINDSTROM

UNIVERSITY OF CALIFORNIA PRESS
BERKELEY AND LOS ANGELES 1958

University of California Press
Berkeley and Los Angeles, California

Cambridge University Press
London, England

Printed in the United States of America

ACKNOWLEDGMENTS

To all those from whom I have been able to learn—teachers, pupils, and friends—I am very happy to express my appreciation and gratitude. I should also like to thank those authors whom I have quoted as references in my notes. The illustrations have been provided by many youngsters, most of whose names are no longer available to me and many of whom are now grown up. I thank them all for their valuable contributions.

The design of the book, as well as continuous aid in its organization and preparation, has been provided by Charles Lindstrom. To Adrian Wilson and Glenn Gosling of the University of California Press I am also grateful for their meticulous care to produce the book as it had been envisioned.

CONTENTS

INTRODUCTION

Psychological inquiry in our century has given new importance to our creation of expressive symbols to relate ourselves meaningfully to other human beings and to the world around us. Uses of verbal language have been most thoroughly examined, but equally rewarding studies in visual symbolism reveal imagery as a basic process of thought, and art as the evidence of this mode by which the individual "realizes" (makes real to himself) his experience. The art of children discloses their characteristic modes of understanding—their visual realizations in imagery—at different stages of their development. From it we can learn much about them and about ourselves.

The illustrations here chosen show this natural development through its successive stages among children I have observed in classes at the San Francisco Museum of Art and especially at the M. H. de Young Memorial Museum in San Francisco during the past eighteen years. Any such selection is necessarily a sampling only, and as each picture is the work of an individual child, it cannot indicate the tremendous range of variation due to personality and other factors that enter into children's art. In using them as "typical examples" of what might be expected from similar groups of unselected children, I realize that hundreds of others—all different—might have served to demonstrate the stages of development discussed here. A teacher is always accumulating large numbers of pictures, discarded or given by such prolific artists, and keeping such a collection within bounds is difficult. Usefulness for illustrating lectures to parents, teachers, and others interested in the art of children has been one of the criteria for keeping a picture. They represent particular instances of their general types.

The point of view held in these classes and presented here is that children have a native ability to express themselves in visual terms just as they have a native ability to express themselves verbally. We may not understand their early scribbling any better than we do their infant babbling, but that does not prove there is no meaning in it for the child himself.

Before a child can speak words that are part of our own vocabulary and combine them in ways which we are capable of comprehending, he must practice making all kinds of sounds, learning gradually the selected repertory of vocables that are used in his hearing. Before a symbol standing for an idea-feeling can be drawn on paper, a child must practice making marks of various kinds. When he invests these marks with meaning they acquire, for him at least, the value of symbols. Will and memory as well as specific muscular controls are exercised. Repetition and selection and, at last, successful communication are the result of persistent effort and incalculable mental energy. Thought and feeling not only accompany each gesture from the beginning but are themselves developed and clarified by the drawing process.[1]

As a child learns to talk he also develops his visual imagery. We can get a glimpse of his view of the world if we look as well as listen. Liveliness of fantasy, dynamic spontaneity, intensity of emotional response, enthusiastic pleasure in making and doing—these are characteristics of the art as well as the speech of children up to the age of seven or so.

Well-known devices for aesthetic effect appear in some of the pictures. Because the teaching of art has traditionally dealt with such matters as color combination and spatial arrangement, it might be thought that painting conventions have been consciously used by the children according to instruction. Actually, the power of certain devices to arouse an aesthetic response in human beings is so elementary, so primitive (or we are) that it operates below rational consciousness. As children use nouns and verbs and exclamations in speaking long before they learn systematic grammar or syntax, so in their picture-making they use the visual terms that suit their immediate expressive purpose.[2]

Purposes change as individuals grow. We express our thoughts and feelings in the words and images at our command. On the other hand, our thoughts and

1

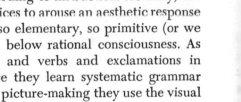

feelings are themselves extended or limited by the wealth and variety or poverty and monotony of the forms in which we can shape them for our comprehension, the symbolic formulations of language and imagery that we can use. Most of us arrive at maturity with purposes that cannot be expressed in the simple speech or drawings that served us as children. Our concepts require more complex symbols and symbolic systems when we make use of verbal and visual means to understand ourselves and each other. Perhaps we shall never use language or vision as poets and painters do, for our purposes may differ from theirs, but as children we were once all artists together. Susanne K. Langer's definition of art as "the creation of forms symbolic of human feeling" is broad enough to include the art of children. Little children's imagery, both verbal and visual, is rich in forms symbolic of human feeling.

"He," she said as she listened to the deep notes of Muldoon the Bassoon, "is right down at the bottom. It's really dark down there." (Quoted in Stanleigh Arnold's report of a four-year-old's reactions to an orchestral recording for children. *San Francisco Chronicle*, September 19, 1954.)

WHAT CHILDREN'S ART MEANS TO CHILDREN

When you visit an art session for nursery school children and see some little person two or three or four years old at an easel busily spreading bright colors with a big brush over a large piece of paper you may wonder what it can mean to him. He is obviously not even trying to represent anything that we can recognize. Presumably, he is just past the stage when he would be trying to get the paint into his mouth, and very likely he is capable still of applying it to his own or his companion's person with as much interest as he takes in "making a picture." What can such activity have to do with art? Why is this daubing and messing around thought to be significant or valuable in any way? A quick glance around at the batch of assorted smears produced by the children fails to disclose any particular "picture" distinguished in any special way from the rest.

If you ask one of the youngest ones what he is doing he is likely to reply simply "Painting," without pausing in his busy brushing. But ask one of the four-year-olds and he will tell you an involved dramatic story full of magic with *non sequiturs* that you would try in vain to connect with what appears on his paper. The room is a babble of voices. Most of the children seem to be talking more to themselves than to each other, and the teacher seems not to have assigned any lesson for the class as a whole.

Plainly, if you want to find out what goes on here, what painting means to these children, you must unobtrusively take a position where you can both listen and observe. Then, though the act appears the same in each instance, the children make themselves known as individuals by the different ways they perform their common act of painting.

Billy, who is only two and a half, seems to have difficulty remembering to dip his brush again in the paint when it is almost dry. His companion, using several colors, ignores the jar of water for cleaning her brush, although the roving teacher pauses from time to time to show the children how to do this. She also points out how a brush full of paint can slip and slide on the paper and does not have to be pressed down on as if it were a crayon of hard material.

Billy's paper is mainly scribbled over, back and forth, with blue except for the parts he hasn't yet attended to. Susan, three years old, puts different wet

colors on top of each other and scrubs them around until she has a muddy soaked area in one part of the paper while the rest remains untouched. Stephen is making bold straight lines, loops, dots, zig-zags, and circles all over his paper, and Ellen is slowly making a long wobbly trail of red that meanders over the separate swatches of yellow and green she has previously painted.

Stephen is an articulate four-year-old who apparently feels very competent in handling the paint brush to make it do what he wants. At any moment one of his circles is likely to acquire a pair of dots for eyes and it will become for him a face. Or one of his straight lines will be attached to the bottom of one of his circles and he will discover that he can now make a flower or a tree. When two straight lines grow from the edge of the circle face, a "man" will appear to him. There are latent possibilities of boxes, ladders, windows, doors, chairs, and flags in the combination of straight lines into rectangular shapes. His first "house" will result from such experiments.

Stephen is about to enter a whole new field of experience: the happy use of simple marks to create pictures figurative in character and schematic in style. He will work in this vein until a desire for more objective realism and a concern for naturalistic visual effects supersede this initial mode a few years hence.

All of the children, at whatever of these preliminary stages, find their work entirely pleasing, although many do not remember which paintings are their own when the class is over. The younger ones seem to be mainly preoccupied with the materials and the physical manipulation of the brush, interested in what happens on the paper when they succeed in combining three factors through their own efforts. (Finger painting, by eliminating the most difficult factor—the brush—is easier; a pencil or wax crayon is usually the first art tool given to children.)

In any case, the picture seems to be only a by-product of the main interest, the *act* of painting. Expressing their feeling-thought about some happening lived or imagined is one of the main uses of art work to children of four and five,[3] but this procedure of "acting-out" a dramatic event is still beyond many of the two- and three-year-old ones. For them, feeling and thinking seem to be directly related to the physical activity going on rather than to mental activity concerned with concepts to be expressed. Their incidental chatter to themselves and each other is not so important as their own performance of an act of skill. They enjoy the "power of being the cause."

Billy's delight is in the blueness of the paint and in

his ability to make more blue appear on the paper before his eyes. Susan is fascinated by what happens when she takes still another color and stirs it into the red and yellow that she has already puddled together. Her triumph will come when she finds that, by using black over all, the remnants of other colors will be effectively obliterated and only black will show. Then she will be ready to go on to other experiments with the materials. Susan, an imaginative child, will probably be inventing stories to accompany her act of painting considerably before her symbols become recognizable to others. Children as young as two will sometimes announce before or after making their scribble what it is about.

The art of painting, as adult artists practice it, is complex—not simply the production of sensations. Their creative processes as well as critical aesthetic judgment are of an order different and far removed

4

from what is possible to children. The beginnings of art for the very young are first of all the learning of muscular control in acquiring a new physical skill and then joyful discovery and wonder in what this skill makes possible to them. Next comes the use of this means to achieve a purpose utterly satisfying to the mind and heart when as narrator and audience of one a child can take out of himself and place in the external world for himself to see and direct the inner drama that *is*, for him, the meaning of a situation experienced and remembered or imagined. Little children do not distinguish as we do between an inner fantasy and an outer "reality." For them, experience of both kinds has the same quality of actual event. Because everything *is* and nothing merely *seems,* a little child does not know when he is pretending or fibbing except as he becomes acquainted with these concepts of his elders, and even then it is not easy to learn to make the distinction in his own thought and action.

Through visual statement, mysteries reach some resolution, reality takes a tangible form, fantasy becomes stated and thereby less confusing, and a small person gains some measure of mastery over the vague but powerful forces that he feels govern his life and his world.' To the extent that magic, animism, and supernaturalism are one's explanations for causes and effects, some method of exorcism is essential until more rational interpretations supply a more comfortable logic to live by. (Adults, who seldom give themselves so completely to any experience as little children do, could not stand the emotional wear and tear of living as they do, so intensely, so passionately, so without perspective or philosophy to sustain them beyond moments regarded not as transitory but as all of life.)

Little children's art provides this means of dealing with phenomena whose complexity needs to be reduced and to be coped with. It provides them, from within themselves, an early sense of human dignity that can eventually grow to great beauty and strength. Although meaning in the symbols of a child's art may be obscure to an adult, it is clear and valid for its maker, who is usually glad to explain it to us so that we may enjoy with him his triumph over chaos.

The process of individuation is a continuous and gradual development within each of us. Several years of puzzlement, inquiry, and experience are needed before a child loses the total egocentricity of the infant and finally realizes that *his* view of things is not *the* view that the world shares, and far, far longer to realize that it is *a* view only. It takes longer still before one can perhaps accept the lonely truth that there is no single view of the world that is shared by everybody.

6

The recognition of personal separateness—of others having their own concepts, different from his, because they see things from their position and condition as individuals and not from his own—is not ordinarily possible before a child is seven. Immaturity in adults reveals itself clearly in the retention of this infantile orientation. The assumption seems to be that, of course, adults are all-knowing and all-powerful and are aware of whatever goes on in one's own thoughts. Presumably all people think and see alike, namely as one does oneself.

An innocent delusion of this kind makes impossible certain other ideas about representation in art. Perspective is not understood, nor chiaroscuro, nor foreshortening, for illusionistic rendering. Every method used by an artist to create realistic effects of distance, volume, surface texture, light and shade as observed in nature, etc., is beyond comprehension to the person who does not know that he can choose one of several alternative positions from which to view a subject, and that each choice offers a different picture. Constancy of size, despite the appearance of diminution with increasing distance, naturalistic proportion without regard to variable emotional significance, the functional relationship of parts to whole in any structure—all such matters are outside the understanding of little children as they might pertain to picture-making; and it is confusing and discouraging when adults object to their disregard for adult convictions and prejudices about appearances in art.

Children see first and picture first separate "things" without regard to contexts. A window conceived as an entity may be drawn sidewise on an area designated as house wall. On a paper lying flat on a table a child may not as a matter of course proceed to paint his picture from our conventional notion of the near edge representing *down* and the far edge *up;* for him, the paper is an undetermined area on which to place his symbols for things. The most commonly seen instance of this sort of nonorientation is perhaps the page of alphabet letters, these scattered about helter-skelter without any reference to left or right, up or down, or any indication of their marching along a horizontal line as we are used to seeing, reading, and writing them. The preschool child sees them and draws them as separate objects. (The *consistent* painting of an entire picture "upside down" by a five-year-old is something I have seen done, as some children reverse left and right when they are first learning to read and write, but I do not see that this practice is analogous. The same boy also painted pictures in the usual way.)

It is the unawareness of being confined within his

own personal view that makes natural those habits of projection and identification and of assertiveness so noticeable in children's verbal and visual expression. Some of their most delightful "works of art" arise from this primitive condition. Innocent of perspective or other conventional "rules" of art, subjective and arbitrary in treatment of color and proportion, discontinuous in thought and lacking relatedness among parts of a whole, these works show us glimpses of a world we ourselves have long since left.[5] It is an art that affects us strangely by its shocking juxtapositions of gaiety and terror, its strong evocative power.

Children gradually become assimilated to the world that spreads out around them. They range farther and farther in the physical environment, and the area of their ideas becomes more extended. To express their concepts visually remains a continuing interest, but communication to others becomes now its major purpose. A large quantity of narrative and descriptive art is produced, covering a multitude of subjects, by nearly every child between the ages of five and eight. Discursive drawing as well as discursive talking takes the place of the early kind of expression.

During this time the schematic mode, using formula images of all sorts, is pushed to the limits of its possibilities for representation. Increasingly, a child's sense of logic, his rational intelligence, comes into play as he tries to make clear his meaning in these pictures. He does not ordinarily judge his own work by aesthetic criteria, "presentational" effectiveness, but seeks naturalistic appearances. Successful communication, for him, requires clarity as to objective facts. He does not spontaneously or consciously try to give us a picture of his inner world but wants to depict accurately some phenomenon of the external physical world. He is also apt to be very disappointed if we cannot read correctly his visual prose description in line and color. If we believe that we can read more and can discern what is sometimes called "the essence of the individual child" revealed in his work, that is no concern of his.

If we can regard the drawings and picture-making of individuals who are not yet adolescent as children's art (however inaesthetic), we must recognize a different mode of thought making itself evident within the two-dimensional schematic style sometime between the ages of seven and ten. If children can be persuaded and encouraged to continue their practice of making visual representations of their ideas through this period and into the next, it is possible that art may become for them a positive value throughout their lifetime. Thought, feeling, and visualization (the ability to picture to oneself) need not become separate, unequally cultivated functions but should remain united in their integrating effect on the mind's maturing.

We do not know reality directly but only by means of concepts we form in our minds. We react then to the feelings those concepts arouse in us. Thus all of our experience is shaped by such concepts as we are able to form and to use. As attention becomes more and more directed outward to the environment during childhood, it seems natural that we should become increasingly perceptive and so seek to modify and correct our primitive concepts in the direction of closer relatedness to what we can observe. We want then that such new understanding as we may acquire be accurate, but we retain still the delusion that we stand face to face with reality. We remain, as children, unaware that our languages, verbal and visual, through which we acquire and present information are symbol systems. We do not realize that they are human inventions by means of which we communicate with one another.

So long as we do not become conscious of the nature of this procedure we are not able consciously to use it for the purposes and in the ways of art. Our picture-making, as our thinking, will continue to be childish until, at whatever age, it becomes clear to us that words are not the things they refer to, images are not what they represent, but both are invented symbols to convey human thought and feeling from the inner to the outer world. The "meaning" of children's art to children might be regarded as means by which they can work through successive stages of development to ways of thinking, feeling, and doing that are adult.

STAGES OF DEVELOPMENT: PART ONE

1. Scribble and chance forms, controlled marks, basic forms, first schematic formulae (ages 2–5)

Observations have been made of little children, infants really, to note their first making of a mark. So far, there seems to be no recorded instance of this act occurring consciously, deliberately, without adult instruction. The baby will grasp a stick or pencil and wave it about, but it is the adult who is present who shows the baby how to make the end of the tool mark in the sand or on the paper. Attention has to be called to this mark that is the effect of the act of pressing and moving the point of the instrument against a surface. The baby, guided in his repetition of this act, quickly learns through imitation how to perform it (and even which end of a pencil is effective) once he learns to look for its "product."

It seems to make no difference whether a child is thus introduced to drawing before or after he begins to talk; scribbling continues to be the kind of drawing done until about the fourth birthday for most children, and scribble of one sort or another continues to be used throughout a lifetime of making marks. We all doodle and cross things out.

The first scribbles are made by swinging the arm back and forth or up and down in an arclike movement. This is varied by a pounding or jabbing movement, resulting in dots or hooks as the point leaves a short trail before the tool is lifted from the paper.

Next come single arcs, still made by the original swinging movement of the arm, but now in one direction only, the tool being lifted at the end of the first stroke instead of being returned to the starting position. This kind of line gradually becomes less curved and from it is derived the intentional horizontal or vertical straight line. A child (and many an adult) will often turn his paper in order to make another horizontal line to serve as a vertical intersecting at right angles the horizontal drawn first, if this type of movement is more easily performed and therefore favored. (According to Dr. Gesell's observations, vertical markings precede horizontal in the sequence of development.)

During the time when single and intersecting straight lines are evolving from the original continuous arc lines of scribble, there appears a kind of spiraling line, more or less dense. Loops, zig-zags, and wavy or jerky trailings are made, but the separate closed circle and the rectangle are not achieved until the time when a child can make separate lines of whatever specific length he determines upon. Scribbling has been his method of acquiring the muscular control needed for the next stage of development.

Now he has the ability he needs to make at will and not by chance the variety of marks that children use for their first schematic symbols, distinguished from scribble, and familiar to us as children's art.

2. Use of repertory for developing formulae (ages 4–6)

Most little children enjoy watching an adult make simple line drawings for their entertainment and will ask for pictures to be made for them—of a man, a house, a dog, a boat, a train. Most adults are pleased to indulge such requests and will fill a sheet of paper with simple schematic representations that satisfy and amuse the child, finally suggesting that the little one do it for himself, using perhaps the already drawn formulae to copy from.

Such exercises in imitation, with help and correction, are a familiar routine of learning that occurs in most families where an infant is a member. It is natural and customary that drawing is introduced in the same way that other skills are. But some advanced scribblers discover for themselves their own ability to invent schematic representations. When this happens, the discovery is much more wonderful and satisfying to the spirit than being trained to repeat a pattern made by someone else. Independent creation is a joy of a very special quality. The squares, circles, and various lines of scribble suggest to the mind, when it is ready, *images,* so that with slight additions or modifications these can be converted to figures that stand for concepts in the child's own mind.

Having recognized this delightful possibility, the shaping of concepts is given impetus as the child now sets out purposefully to make the figure again, choosing from his repertory only those marks that are needed and leaving out miscellaneous scribble. In this way he arrives at his first formula figure—a schema that he can repeat as often as he chooses. Although the human being is usually the first such invention, others are also frequent, and the first is rapidly followed by others. Flowers and trees are represented by combinations of dense spiral scribble or circles with attached straight lines for stems or trunks; houses, windows, doors, flags, etc., are simply made up of rectangles and straight lines. Outlines of such basic shapes are often filled in with solid scribble of one or more colors.

A schema to stand for the concept "man" will usually be developed by a child in several ways if he is left free to explore the possibilities available to him and is not dependent on a single formula received ready-made from someone else. The type of figure that he finally settles on by preference and continues then to use for the next few years will be his own unique creation.[6] The various "people" drawn by the individuals of a children's class are distinguishable as the inventions of their different originators. A child who makes his figures with long thin open bodies and single line legs keeps to this general style; a child who has hit upon a rake-type form as solution to the problem of indicating hands or feet uses it consistently and does not adopt the button or fan form that another child may have devised. (Picture 12.) Animals are shown in profile, constructed in a mode similar to that used by the individual child for his human beings.

A similar individuality of style appears in the schemata for houses. Each child is his own architect: the gable roof design with two windows and a door is not used by the child whose houses are flat-roofed and one-windowed. If spiral scribble smoke comes out of the chimney, it will always go straight up in one child's picture and to the right in another's.

Boats, bridges, and vehicles are other structures that appear among the early schemata and retain their basic form through whatever refinements may come in their development.

First schemata for flowers and trees, however, are almost identical among the children's representations. (Picture 10.) They soon become varied in form as leaves are added, tree trunks thickened, daisy or tulip shapes evolved from the undifferentiated spiral scribble or simple circle used at first. The trees sometimes have thick short trunks with a multitude of radiating single line branches sprouting from what looks like a sawed-off top, or they bear fruit evenly spaced around the perimeter of the circular mass of foliage. As with the figures for people and houses, the schemata for trees are individually formulated concepts varying from child to child.

A child may work on the development and elaboration of one or several of these symbols over a consid-
erable length of time, covering sheets of paper with
his many examples of the same subject or a jumbled
assortment of several, along with some miscellaneous
scribbling. At this stage a child's picture often shows
a collection of unrelated ideas, a sampling of many
enterprises in formula making. These are all rapidly
executed, not patiently toiled over, and each "picture"
is finished within a very few minutes.[7] (It is not uncommon, however, for a child younger than four, who
does not yet make schemata, happily to scribble and
scrawl in dreamy fashion for a long time on a single
sheet of paper without feeling at any moment that he
has "finished" his picture.)

Many four-year-olds and most five-year-olds have
perfected to their own satisfaction, through such practice, a repertory of several symbols that they take pride
in and that they can use readily and exactly. They
often like to see these figures clearly and neatly set
forth, one at a time, without irrelevant markings on
the paper. The concept is definite, competently executed, and if they can draw the letters of their name as
well, this is all that they feel belongs in their finished
picture.

For a while they remain content to produce these
finished and isolated examples of accomplishment and
skill. But it is not long before a more elaborate picture
appears. Indeed, some very young children (of four
and five) hasten to make a complex use of their rudi-
mentary first schemata in compositions that describe
an event or a scene. Combinations of tree and house,
flower and shining sun, person in boat, etc., do occur

often before the individual schemata used have become perfected or "set." (Picture 3.)

By six, children generally are ready to make a picture of anything that can be thought of, composing it with combinations of the schemata they command and creating new schemata as occasion requires, filling in with verbal narrative the action that is not clearly pictured. One little girl of six explained her picture of a confetti-dotted arc as "the world and everything in it." (Plate 2.)

Picture 6, a locomotive painted by a five-and-a-half-year-old boy, is an example of an already achieved single schema, while picture 13, by a boy one year younger, shows an early attempt to draw a locomotive with the engineer in his cab before a schema for either of the two concepts has been established. In this case there is really a larger single concept embracing two parts in a clear relationship.

In the parade of animals (picture 14) we see a single formula—a four-legged animal shape—adapted to represent elephant, camel, and giraffe by the addition of trunk, hump, or neck as the distinguishing feature permitting identification. The little girl (picture 4) standing between two black raining clouds conforms to the usual representation of a little girl by the child who painted this picture. The clouds with their pendants of raindrops are a new invention appearing here for the first time. It is to be expected that this symbol for a rain cloud, shown twice here, will appear again in other pictures by this child during the next half year or so.

Pictures 7 and 8 show the use of formula figures in serial combination. The Maypole subject is a fairly simple picture based on repetition of the established schema for "person"; the landscape makes use of several different schemata in a more complicated sequence: house, trees, flowers, swings, and slide all embraced by a formal linear rainbow below a dark blue sky.

14

3. Whatever can be thought of can be pictured (ages 5–8)

Through the years five to eight children make hundreds of pictures by combining their rehearsed and perfected schemata to describe situations or events. The picture may become a subject for frequent repetition, as the earlier separate schemata were, until it too can be made readily in its final form. There is a period of experimentation and variation until the preferred version is decided upon; refinement and elaboration of detail follow; and at last comes the definitive composition of the theme, which is likely to become frozen and invariable no matter how often it is repeated.[8] A kind of automatism may set in, with a careless sort of shorthand indication of the well-worn formula representation when thought and action are not closely connected during the drawing. When children engage in stereotype production, this seems to me to be a manifestation of the well-recognized conservatism and ritualism evident in other fondnesses for exact repetition of familiar forms: the exact words of a familiar story, the accented rhythm of verse or song, or the undeviating order of accustomed acts in the performance of daily routines. We may find the monotony tedious, but it apparently satisfies a need in the child. Is the vividness of imagery itself hypnotic, and does the eventual "fixing" of it provide freedom of the mind to wander off to other matters? Perhaps the defining of a category is so pleasing a form of security that it serves as a refuge: the known.

In addition to the work of perfecting one or more "set" pictures that can be produced whenever wished, children between the ages of five and eight picture anything they are able to think of—remembered or imagined. Undaunted by subjects that professional artists would hesitate to attempt, they are prepared to picture every idea, whether or not it is one that adults are easily capable of visualizing. Lack of understanding does not keep them from symbolizing even some very abstract concepts in visual forms as their minds are able to associate very widely and loosely among slight similarities or analogies and can make large inclusions and vast omissions of the relevant where we would distinguish differences. (As a baby learning to talk is likely to call all animals "dog," so the same formula figure may serve as horse or dog or cat for the five-year-old picture maker.) Logic and consistency, the dualism of an inner world of fantasy distinguished from an outer world of fact, do not stand as obstacles in the way of children's free creation. If a recognized difficulty should arise they can usually contrive a way around it that will satisfy their own requirements—of which plausibility to an adult mind may not be one.[9] This ready inventiveness seems to me to be related to the juvenile requirement for cause for every phenomenon. (Cf. Piaget, *The Child's Conception of the World.*) In the absence of knowledge, it is necessary to invent or refer to magic or supernaturalism in order to secure *some* explanation, however fantastic, for everything.

Perception is limited by interest, and interest at this stage is likely to focus on one thing at a time, single units in the picture. It is further limited by subjective, emotional emphasis or selection of parts of the unit which are felt to be important. Other parts are ignored as irrelevant to the childish concept. One result of this mode of thought at this period in art is the established schema to stand for each concept. Another result is a static type of composition for the picture in which each item is shown as a thing in itself, not required to adapt itself to other things present so as to function organically within the whole picture. The effect is as of a sum in addition or a listing in a catalogue.

We are sometimes given the impression of elaboration rather than simplification, as in some of the early drawings of the Golden Gate Bridge, an impressive visual experience to children of the San Francisco region. In these pictures we must look through the apparent image to see how much and how drastically our concept of this great suspension bridge has been reduced to the simple notion of a horizontal span. Although the child has actually seen and indicated more than this, the structure is not rationally comprehended; the more-than-this is merely decoration without function, an impression of size and gay color, a happy experience to make a picture about. Experience significant to the child in his *feeling* relation to his environment is what happens to him or what he can cause to happen, and this is his motivation for art activity. Expressive purpose determines how he will narrate or describe the experience.

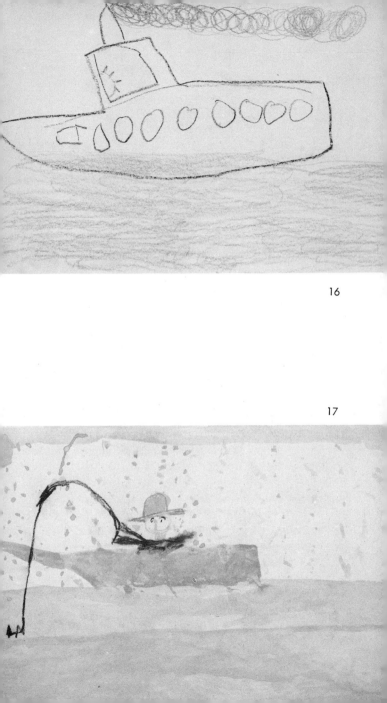

4. Development of possibilities within the schematic mode (ages 7–10)

Children seven to nine or ten years old usually have several favorite subjects in their repertory (but often only one or two). As time goes on they are often thought to be in a rut because of their preference for continuing to make "the same old picture" instead of inventing new themes. They may seem much less bold and adventurous in their art than they have been in the past. Actually, most of them have been quietly extending their skill, working out many difficult problems within the limitations of their schematic mode and attempting solutions to problems of representation that lie outside its rigid boundaries. Within their pictures are to be found many evidences of patient experiment and ingenious modifications and adjustments worked out to accommodate their increasing demand for naturalistic representation.

By this time they have devised their own characteristic representations of many things in nature and for certain man-made structures. People can be shown in several stiff positions intended to indicate action; they can be drawn in profile views that still retain a certain frontality of torso; costuming of a specific role aids in identifying the actors of a scene which is furnished with its necessary props. Animals (still customarily in profile) are differentiated as to species and no longer figure as indeterminate quadrupeds. Color is used more naturalistically, less fancifully, than it has been before and background features are introduced: a range of mountains, the sea, a rainbow bridging the space between sky and earth. Although the custom of lining things up on a ground line near the bottom of the picture or on the edge of the paper itself still persists, the usual strip of blue sky across the top with the usual yellow sun is often replaced now by rain, clouds, stars, snowflakes, or sunsets. Or the sky color is brought all the way down to the ground line.

Most children still make no attempt to model forms or show light and shade, although a few cast shadows or reflections in water may occur in their pictures. Some have learned to indicate distance between near and far figures by raising the ground line in order to show smaller figures beyond nearby ones. The use of more than one ground line for this purpose often appears. There is also the overlapping of figures to the rear by those in front, although the preference remains to let each item stand in its own separate space.

No systematic use of perspective is made, but there

18

are a number of ingenious ways of showing difficult
views without this means. Both sides of a street, with
houses and flowering trees, are indicated by the use
of two ground lines. One can see what is on one side
of the street by holding the paper up in one direction,
and what is on the other side of the street by turning
the paper so that the other side is up. Verticals generally, in such complex views where ground plan and
elevation are meant to be seen, appear to have been
flattened out to a horizontal position, as in the pictures showing fence posts, pier pilings, hopscotch
players, etc.[10] (Pictures 18, 19, 22; plate 11.)

No very serious interest is yet apparent in modifying
the customary disproportion of parts in the formula
figures that have served for so long. But there is a very
definite concern for adjusting the comparative sizes
of the different items in a picture, so that people are
no longer bigger than their houses, and flowers do
not grow to the height of trees. All elements of the
picture are logically interrelated now, in their meaning if not in accordance with "conventional rules" of
composition.

The cat who walks onto the page (picture 15) and
the little herd of horses (plate 6) are animals not to be
mistaken as to species, and there is even some degree
of characterization present in their indicated movement. Naturalistic color is an important factor in the
pastoral scene.

In plate 7 the kite-flying boy is in action and shown
partly in profile, as is the woman watering the flower
in plate 9. This latter picture is typical of the kind in
which views inside and outside the house or barn are

19

shown simultaneously. Both make use of an *area* of ground and of an area of sky instead of a simple line as base and top.

A very pleasing decorative picture of a house (plate 10) is not a deliberately contrived stylized design but rather an earnest attempt to describe the subject factually. If the boy could only have found a way of showing the fourth side of the house as well, he would have done so. As it is, both ends and one side are shown and the house is set *within* a fenced area. Each strip of fence is shown as if faced directly (as is each side of the house), and the fence is understood as continuing behind the house. Three-dimensionality is striven for within the possibilities of the style. Gate, window shutters, and base line of the house hint at partial perspectival solutions.

The girls playing hopscotch (plate 11) require three separate views: directly facing the player, directly facing the three waiting players, and looking directly down on the marked-out game pattern on the ground. Nothing in this rendering of figures in space hints at the need for a system of representation different from what has been suitable for simpler pictures of silhouette shapes standing along a base line.

Picture 18 includes foreground, middle distance, and background and shows interest in receding forms in space and a need for a more effective technique to accomplish what is wanted. The vertical supports for the pier over the water, extending as they do here in a horizontal direction, are not "right" in the opinion of their maker, nor is the garden patch that refuses to lie down properly on the ground. The method he is accustomed to using will no longer serve for what his purposes have become.

Pictures 20, 21, 22, and 23 are samples of the work of Susan representative of the kind of visual representation she used during four consecutive years. The first, done when she was six, shows some of the typical devices of picture-making at that age. People, tree, and house are lined up along the bottom edge of the paper. The forms are simple and clear in silhouette, shaped with the primitive emphasis on contrast of direction (arms extend at right angles from bodies, chimney projects from roof slope at right angle to base, hats sit squarely on or over heads, tree rises in exact verticality to paper edge as ground line). Each shape has been drawn in line and filled in solidly with crayon of the same color as the outline. Each thing stands separately in its own allotted space. Each is a schema or formula image that stands for this particular child's idea of how a tree, a house, or a person may be pictured. As such, they are parts of her own repertory

20

21

for picture-making and appear over and over again in different combinations to represent different themes and events. They may be drawn small or large, according to the picture space available, but their relative sizes within the pictures are not determined by naturalistic proportion. (The house—a separate thing in itself—does not have to have a door large enough for the people to enter.) The umbrellas are supposed to be directly over the heads and Susan knows that umbrella handles are centered, but her people do not yet have elbow joints and so must hold their umbrellas as they do, arms extended, handles grasped, heads sheltered from the rain.

Picture 21 shows members of Susan's class at school doing their Maypole dance. Seven years old now, she continues to place the figures on the ground line, the bottom edge of the paper. Each person pictured stands specifically for one of her classmates, whom she names in discussing her picture. The varicolored ribbons have been definitely assigned, as in class. The schema for person is much the same as it has been, but some of the arms bend now and the colors of hair, skin, and clothing are differentiated in the interest of greater naturalism and factual representation. This picture shows eye and mouth in the profile faces, but curiously leaves the others without features.

When Susan was eight, her interest in accurate representation while still working within the schematic mode led her to use many of the methods that are commonly adopted by children at this stage of visualization. Picture 22 is an example of the two-ground-line device. Her subject was the street where she lived and she drew this as a black strip running up the length

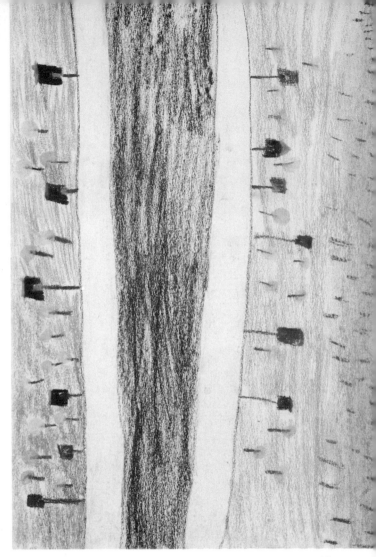

of the paper in the middle. Giving the paper a quarter turn to the right, she drew the houses with their walks or driveways, lawns and flowering trees as they would be seen along one side of the street. Turning to see (and picture) the houses, lawns, and trees on the opposite side of the street was accomplished by turning the paper and drawing above the second ground line. In looking at the picture, we are supposed to do this turning of it so that an upright view of the things shown is possible.

The fourth picture of Susan's series was done when she was nine. By this time she had entered the intermediate class at the museum and was having her first experiences in drawing from observation. She had drawn in the tea garden more than once and brought in this picture done from memory at school. In it there is now a foreground occupied by the reflecting pool and goldfish. The raised ground line from which trees and shrubs grow is marked by a bamboo fence. For the first time, although the crayon rendering still uses outline and flat two-dimensional forms, there is the indication of depth by the use of overlapping shapes, so that some are seen to be behind others and each does not stand isolated in silhouette.

Typical renderings of the Golden Gate Bridge subject at this time illustrate the kinds of changes and clarification of concepts that take place in children's art during this stage. This famous suspension bridge, painted a bright orange red, can be seen easily from many parts of the city. It is used familiarly and frequently, I believe, by almost all San Franciscans, and even very young children include it naturally among the things they know. It is a frequent subject of their drawings and paintings from the age of five on. The series here illustrates some of the ways they think about the Golden Gate Bridge.

Even the most elementary concept (picture 24) has the bridge colored orange and crossing the water. In this picture it is supported by three piers unrelated to the towers above. The loop or swag of the cable is shown as several diagonals descending from tower tops to handrail. The vertical posts on the bridge have no reference to actuality. The importance of the railing may be due to its continuing nearby presence just beyond the window as one travels by car across the bridge.

In picture 25 the bridge is carried by two heavy piers but there are no towers from which the cable might be strung. The vertical cables are present, however, connecting top and bottom. A ship passing beneath the bridge is a frequent additional feature of bridge pictures.

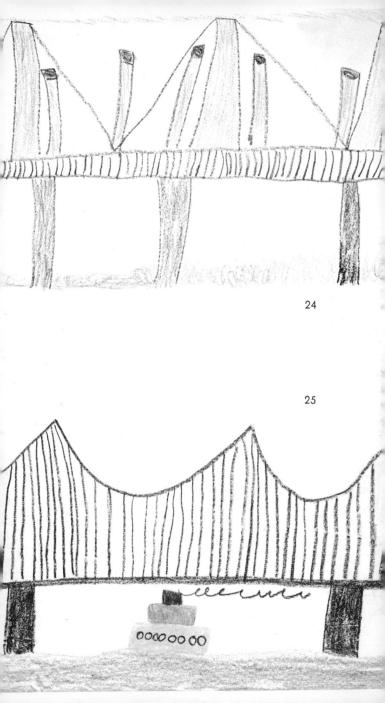

24

25

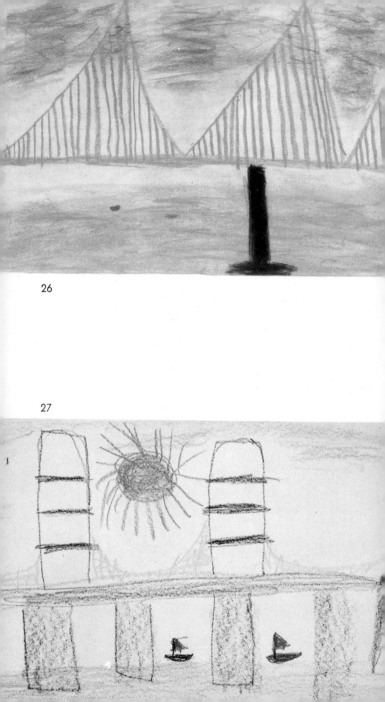

26

27

Picture 26 gives a view far out into the Pacific and the western sky streaked with the sunset. The boat is a long way out beyond the bridge and so appears very small. This is the one picture of the series done by a girl (age 7). She, too, makes additional peaks on her bridge, holds it up with a single solid black pier, and omits the structurally essential pair of towers.

Picture 27, by a six-year-old boy, shows us the broad and open face of the towers as they are seen when one is *on* the bridge. Supports below are many and heavy, leaving room for passage of only small sailing boats. Cables are loosely strung and tangled but do have a kind of low suspension from the towers.

If the child who painted picture 28 had only continued his towers downward into the water instead of planting them on the bridge, his rendering would be plausible. The roadway, however, does connect with solid ground on either side and can carry a truck. The truck driver will come to the toll gate on the San Francisco side. This is an eight-year-old's representation, still within the simple post and lintel concept of building, as with blocks.

Children, before they reach the age of nine, can understand the bridge as *hung* by the cables which are held aloft by towers rising vertically and continuously from foundations in the earth. In picture 29 of the series there is only one long loop shown between the two towers and it is fair to assume that the boy knows that the longitudinal cables are anchored to left and right (outside the picture space). In order to show traffic on the bridge he had to reduce the number of vertical cables, but the principle of their function is clear. His fishing boat below may be out of scale, but it is manned by a person who shows articulation of parts.

PLATE 1

PLATE 2

PLATE 3

PLATE 4

PLATE 5

PLATE 6

PLATE 7

PLATE 8

PLATE 9

PLATE 10

PLATE 11

PLATE 12

PLATE 13

PLATE 14

PLATE 15

28

29

AESTHETIC CONCERNS AND INSTANCES OF EXCEPTIONAL DEVELOPMENT

Occasionally, children of all ages enjoy occupying themselves with pure design. Their art is not limited to the figurative. Arrangements of colors, lines, and shapes that are symmetrically placed on the paper or that rhythmically repeat a simple motif are used instead of a pictorial subject.

Pictorial subjects, too, may be presented in so balanced and formal a composition as to suggest that the child's interest and taste turn toward the creation of an ordered harmony in thought, feeling, and expression. His visual descriptions and dramas then reveal clarity, subtlety, and singleness of mood that are the result of an integrating principle at work throughout. The relationships among the various elements of his picture are nicely adjusted by his aesthetic awareness. Themes chosen for such pictures often have to do with nature in various "moods" or seasonal effects felt as emotionally significant. The conscious purpose informing such works and the successful achievement of this purpose give aesthetic value to the pictures. Works of this kind are the usual prize winners when misguided adults stage children's art contests, introducing the competitive motive where it does more harm than good.[11]

Precocity of various kinds and varying degrees is exhibited by a few individuals in almost any group of children. When it is of an order so rare and original as to be entirely unexpected, an experienced teacher might well believe it a manifestation of genius. Two of the many hundreds of children whose art work I have had the opportunity to observe seemed exceptional in these ways: they were able to conceive and create images much more complex than could be achieved by others of their age, and they were extraordinarily perceptive of both objective fact and subjective effect. Their drawings indicated a clear sense of structure in the interrelationships of parts and also showed the artist's appreciation of significant, expressive gesture or attitude so that the total concept declared its affective meaning.

Dennis' lion (picture 30) turns his head to us and lifts it in a roar. The great mane, sharp teeth, long bared claws, and flicking tail are vividly expressive. Not only is the animal drawn from the difficult front view rather than an easier profile position, but the distance between fore and hind legs is convincingly shown by their placement beneath the foreshortened body. The whole figure was drawn in vigorous confidence with a sure and rapid line, after a moment or two of thought on the subject of what is to be seen at the zoo. Other drawings by this same little boy during the time that I knew him were equally original and impressive. Dennis was five years old then and possessed a power for graphic expression that would be beyond most of us at any age.

Leslie was seven when her mother asked if Leslie might not come to the intermediate class with her older brother because she was especially fond of drawing and might do better in that class than in the one for her own age group. Reluctantly (because this is not an uncommon request and does not usually work out successfully) I agreed that she might try the observation course with the understanding that if she were not really ready for it she would wait until she was older before joining this class as a regular member. This was a most interesting and surprising experiment, for Leslie was indeed able to accomplish every assignment with skill and comprehension equal to that of the ten- and eleven-year-old students and surpassing the ability of the new nine-year-old class members. During her free choice periods, her wide range of subjects chosen for picturing indicated a fertile imagination, a vivid recall of sensed qualities in things seen and remembered, and great resourcefulness in invention. (Pictures 31, 32, 33, 34, and 35.)

My impression of both Leslie and Dennis was of keen intellect, alert sensitivities, disciplined energy, and a generous unspoiled readiness to respond to

whatever challenge was offered as a welcome new experience. These children displayed the poise and competence and quiet self-reliance of superior individuals at ease in a world that was stimulating, intensely interesting, and ready to their grasp. I think their habit of success, their easy comprehension, and their relative freedom from some of the ordinary frustrations most children have to cope with made learning and doing especially delightful to them.

Color plate 1, of a rectangle enclosing square and circular shapes, I regard as exceptionally pleasing. It appears "composed" as few of these first essays in controlled marks are. The work is by a four-year-old girl.

34

35

Plates 12, 13, and 14 are examples of aesthetic use of color, form, and space relationships in the work of children six to nine years old.

The rainbow over the brown hump of a hill and the few scattered raindrops (plate 12) express in minimum basic visual terms the concept of sunshine returning as a shower ends; the pleasurable feeling we have all experienced on seeing a landscape so illuminated is implicit in this primer version of the event. Similarly, the happy child in the falling snow (plate 13) presents herself as simply enjoying the phenomenon. Snow is a rare and memorable event in the San Francisco area. She stands, smiling, warmly dressed for the weather, and shows us her delight.

An "abstract design," such as plate 14 illustrates, sometimes is a picture intended to be representational. In this instance, the black line is a roadway crossing a stream and the different fields of the countryside are distinguished by different colors.

STAGES OF DEVELOPMENT: PART TWO

1. Dissatisfaction with limitations of the schematic mode (ages 8–12)

When a child of eight or nine paints a "tree" that someone else derides, or when he wishes to draw something that he believes he cannot, the fear of failure or ridicule will often prevent his attempting what he would very much like to do. Discontented with his own accomplishments and extremely ambitious to please others with his art, he tends to give up original creation and personal expression in favor of routine copying. Further development of his visualizing powers and even his capacity for original thought and for relating himself through personal feeling to his environment may be blocked at this point. It is a crucial stage beyond which many adults have not advanced. (In the use of verbal language the corresponding level is that in which slang and hackneyed clichés are made to serve for all communication of thought and feeling. Thought and feeling themselves then, I should suppose, become banal as they are constricted and conformed to these common molds.)

A number of factors contribute to such a stultifying impasse. Most important among them, it seems to me, are certain quite natural tendencies that both teachers and parents recognize as generally characteristic, however deplorable, of the ages between nine and twelve. In our culture children at this time become aggressively competitive within their own circle or pack. Antagonism between boys and girls is usual. They are apt to be resistant to adult authority, active and adventurous in physical exploits, pitifully eager for the admiration of their peers, and contemptuous of those younger or older than themselves. They are loyal to the conventional mores and respectful of the taboos of their own group. The effort to achieve acceptable conformity within their own young society proceeds against an uneasy but persistently growing genuine awareness of personal individuality. Such awareness tends to be suppressed, not acknowledged except as the child can manage to distinguish himself among rivals for popularity by a display of skill in one of their accepted activities.

All these socially motivated herd drives effectively inhibit the previous egocentric self-confidence in spontaneous expression and imaginative creation. The kind of self-confidence that belongs to civilized maturity is not yet within reach of these children who can no longer enjoy the infantile variety. Their earlier originality is now regarded by the children themselves as error, incompetence, embarrassing naïveté. Having attained the level of barbarism they are ashamed of their recent more primitive innocence. Many of them are capable of becoming civilized if they are not held back.

Interest in objective reality, a concern for facts, and a materialist utilitarian approach toward actualities of the physical environment make for the children now a new orientation. It may seem to be a period of aesthetic dormancy for many boys and girls.

For the art teacher who can accept this condition and recognizes, too, that it is a period of increasingly rational perception, there are opportunities to stimulate a student's efforts to visualize. The cultivation of this ability is essential to both the appreciation and the creation of art that may come later. Other areas of interest and activity also are dependent on this particular ability of human beings to visualize. Its development can be encouraged and guided within the particular interests and potentialities of the children when they are ready, even though their exercises may not result at this time in anything that could be called art.

Children who find their primitive formula symbols inadequate to express what they now wish to communicate need assistance in arriving at more complex

38

and more satisfactory symbols. In order for them to produce the new realism that they crave but do not yet understand, they need to be given direct assistance in the form of demonstration and common-sense explanation of principles that condition structure, function, and especially vision. Eager for understanding and able now to follow logical analysis, they need to have attention drawn to what is observable, what can be perceived, in the visible world around them. They can be shown how things work and how artists make different kinds of representations of things. They can even accept as reasonable that different artists might be perceiving different things than they themselves would in looking at an object.

The practice of intensive looking—together with trying to imagine how it might *feel* if one were to become the object being studied, for the purpose of finding true relationships within the motif—is an exercise that makes constructive use of children's abilities and interests at this time. Their very obsession with substance, their materialist bias are adequate motivation for them to learn prosaic technical aspects of art. In learning to observe, curiosity about facts is very useful.

Everyday subjects found in the visible sensible world around us can serve for the practice of observation. Regardful attention to the fundamental relations within any structure is an absorbing task of search and discovery. We shall no longer find in the children's art such things as a tree full of four-legged bluebirds! Setting down on paper here what has been discerned there makes looking a purposeful and disciplined study. It engages the student in an experience of concentration that counters some of the diffuse and distracted ways of his life. Many children today show the effects of overstimulation in their dependence on continuous entertainment and happenings outside themselves. A successful communication of understanding is the result of earnest and intelligent effort. When subjects for such study have been selected for aesthetic value and interest the project may somewhat affect the growth of desirable sensitivities.

Children of this age left to themselves without any guidance of their peculiar proclivities seldom improve their drawing skill relative to their advancing mental powers. As they turn their undiscriminating attention to facts of their visual environment they are attracted by what is conspicuous or obviously aimed at their immature sensibilities. A large part of their visual environment consists of movies, television, comics, and commercial illustration. All pictures are lumped, for them, in the category of art, and what they themselves would like to achieve in their own art is a degree of realism equal to the most illusionistic representation. (Their acceptance of the socially "given," their cataloguing of appearances are aspects of "almanac factualism" which lie between savage animism and scientific consciousness in the development of human concepts.) They find it easier, however, to make copies of simple cartoon stereotypes done in the schematic mode they have been accustomed to use in their own drawing. Assuming to themselves now a more participative social role they adopt as ideals the crude, lively, and vulgar versions of beauty, fame, wealth, power, and success that are popularly symbolized in this mode.

Because such familiar schemata are recognized readily by everybody and are the inventions of commercial artists who are well paid to produce them, they have for children a compelling validity as art which is absent from any original imagery of their own creation. Anyone, however, who will practice, over and over again, the physical movements of making a simple line tracing or copy will be able to do it accurately and almost automatically after a while. No thinking, no ability beyond patience and persistence are needed to acquire the mechanical skill of this "art." No learning to use one's faculties constructively, creatively, to reach further or to grasp more surely an understanding and appreciation of human potentialities takes place.

But to become so skilled brings ready acclaim from others as ignorant as and less diligent than oneself. It is gratifying to the juvenile ego to bask in the delusion of possessing "artistic talent," until the means of

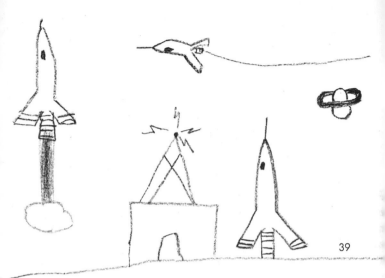

obtaining such pleasurable recognition becomes too boring to intelligence. Then the young "artist" gives up forever the tedium of "art" without ever having come close to experiencing art. Among the other children of the group in which such virtuosity flourishes, a parallel delusion takes hold: that they have no talent, that there's no use in their studying art because they "never could draw."

Art teachers deplore copying because it is motivated by these widely held delusions that perpetuate a whole series of mistaken notions and false evaluations concerning art. "Art" is being used as an instrument for self-display. As such it is bound to be spurious. Admiration for effects obtained by superficial manual dexterity, as though this trained facility in itself were all of art, encourages a cheap and trashy taste. It obscures understanding and genuine appreciation of artists and their serious work. It also makes more difficult the real task of learning that has been bypassed and must be returned to by the student. A teacher would much prefer to undertake the instruction of those other students who are addicted to Technology and The Horse than to have the task of helping a student build his genuine foundation of understanding beneath the copyist's trivial display of glib know-how.

Technology and The Horse are two curiously common enthusiasms of children within the nine-to-twelve-year age range, although these subjects as special favorites often appear at an earlier and sometimes continue to a later time. They seem to satisfy what might be called romancing idealism at a time when fantasying and imagining are somewhat feeble. Boys often specialize in drawing vehicles—ships, trucks, tanks, and especially airplanes, with emphasis on military and naval models. Rockets, flying saucers, and spaceships for interplanetary travel are more recent variations on this standard theme (as bomb explosions are now to some extent replacing the traditional volcanoes in scenes of violent destruction).

Some boys are mildly obsessed by horses, but this subject seems to be more favored by girls, a few of whom seem so passionately devoted to the idea of this splendid creature that they cannot give their minds to any other drawing subject. They show a loving attention to the possibilities in the form. Instead of developing a single stereotype representation they strive continually to improve and vary their renditions. Their concern for detail and for showing different aspects of the subject is equal to that of the boys enthralled by machines of transport.

Juvenile idealism is indicated in the human types children prefer to draw at this time, these being quite rigidly stereotyped. By adult standards the ideals appear grotesque. The girls have certain notions of feminine beauty as represented in the "glamorous" face—large-eyed, snub-nosed, red-mouthed, and practically chinless. Eyelashes are very important features. Hair is added on top and at the sides of the masklike face in elaborate arrangements without regard to any plausible head shape, often being squared-off in corners above the loop outline of the face. Bodies exist, if at all, small in proportion to the face and only for wearing a two-dimensional dress design; arms and legs, tiny hands and feet are as ineffectual as possible. A common complaint of girls at this age is that they cannot draw men or that their boys look like girls.

Boys of this age rarely even attempt to include a female figure in their pictures. The men they draw are usually "rough-tough" types, frequently along the lines

40

of the Dick Tracy concept of manliness. As with the girls' drawings of people, these, too, show dwarfing of bodies and limbs in favor of large stupid faces. Domestic life has no interest as theme for most boys; action and adventure and criminal ferocity predominate if human beings appear at all in their pictures.

A kind of neutral theme in this sexual differentiation of interest is the landscape or pastoral subject. All of the children paint the out-of-doors in scenes that they can imagine. The boys tend to more purely pictorial drama in their stronger and more dynamic compositions; the girls are apt to make weak and simple indications of beaches, mountains, fenced fields, and farm buildings for a quiet picture involving people as the general subject. A common preference for the exotic or romantic landscape leads to the picturing of scenes long ago or far away. (Plate 15.)

2. A program for sustaining interest (ages 9–11)

I do not mean to categorize bluntly the children, who are all individuals and whose interests are by no means identical. Many do not exhibit the common biases that have been mentioned here and some are aesthetically alert. In order to devise a course of instruction that would take into account the needs and the interests observed, it is helpful to be acquainted with what might reasonably be expected, and I have found that aesthetic interest is generally at low ebb in the years of childhood immediately preceding puberty. What students in an

My Mother

art class are able to learn depends in large measure on individual background and previous conditioning of attitude. Therefore, a course designed for presentation at the nine-through-eleven-year level needs to be adapted for individual differences as these make their appearance among the students. Flexibility and ingenuity on the part of the teacher would suggest ways of presenting such a course in places other than an art museum.

Depending on the number of children nine to eleven years old who register for this course at the museum, it is given once or twice a week after school and again in the summer vacation period. Twenty students make a good size for the class. Assistance is needed if there are more.

The first day's assignment is a drawing from memory of each child's own house. Also, a portrait of father, mother, or other member of the household and of any pet animal that the child may have or wish to have.

From the children's remarks and the difficulties en-
countered in drawing these subjects, it is decided
whether the next session will be spent on studying
anatomy or perspective. Most of the work of the se-
mester will be in observing and drawing structures:
natural forms of creatures and plants, or man-made
objects.

As most of the children are accustomed to drawing

from memory or imagination, the first assignment is not especially difficult except as it challenges them to be specific instead of general in their image reference. Immediately after class, they have the opportunity and an incentive to look more closely than usual at what they have tried to remember and to see what they have not before seen in the visually familiar. They will note the number of windows their house has, and observe how Mama wears her hair. (Picture 41.)

It often happens that we do not consciously look at and perceive what is visually taken for granted, and we do not ordinarily have any particular reason to make a deliberate check on our memories of this kind. Some students come back to class the following week with drawings of these same subjects that they have made at home. When they do this, the second drawings show a great increase in observation over the ones done from memory in class. These first attempts to draw from a model or a motif make them eager for more of this new kind of art experience. Children respond to the challenge of making responsible statements.

A number of sessions are spent in the classroom, studying the human figure in its varying proportions and its possible movements. The children test the effect of position changes. They test the ways their own

limbs operate through different gestures and balance shifts. These they can demonstrate to themselves. Then, as a model for his classmates, each takes a brief turn at holding a pose while the rest draw.

Sometimes sculptures are used for anatomical analysis and for more lengthy poses than can be asked of a student. In both cases, emphasis is kept on observing proportion and relationship of parts within the whole. The dynamics of physical cause and effect, which explain in objective terms such matters as directions of movement, gesture, and balance, are apparent in the model to pupils who are learning simple empathy through processes of identification with the model and projection of their own response as this becomes clear to them. They are encouraged to feel the pull on the hoe, or the push on the broom, etc., as one of them dramatizes an action in front of the class. Whether the drawing time is brief or extended, finicking with details is discouraged. An occasional series of action poses for the purpose of drawing the "action" rather than the form counteracts the tight and static thinking and drawing habits that inhibit the children's development toward greater freedom. (Picture 42.)

The same principle of discerning and describing the dynamic integration of the figure or form, without regard to surface pattern, is maintained when the class is taken to draw animals at the Academy of Sciences' natural history museum nearby. (Pictures 44, 45, 46.) This is done to help the children outgrow what their art has thus far largely been (and what they themselves now dislike in it): the primitive two-dimensional depiction of shapes by outline and the filling-in of surfaces treated flatly. Their pictures in this style are

44

45

ANTELOPE

decorative in design but irrational or inorganic in construction. The children object to the very qualities that adults find aesthetically pleasing. They are ambitious to overcome an habitual style which obstructs their purpose and is felt to be inappropriate to their current thought and taste. Education of their feelings, helping them to establish emotional rapport with what is regarded as exterior to themselves, is in order.[12] But it can only accompany, not substitute for, the rational understanding which is so eagerly sought.

The study of form and of structure includes observations of nature out-of-doors in areas of the park adjoining the museum. Here it is possible to take notice of the effects of wind and rain and sun and seasonal change as well as of human purpose, as all these forces work on the living substance of trees and other plants, or on what might be regarded as unchanging stone and wood and earth. Plants are shown to be individual and unique phenomena, each different although retaining the character of its species.

Some sessions are devoted to a study of perspective. The classroom itself is drawn with its doors, walls, floor, and ceiling seen from different locations within the room. Vistas through galleries and corridors, or large glass display cases looked at from different angles, are other ready instances that serve to demonstrate optical effects. People who long for illusionism in their drawings find perspective fascinating. A plumb line, a pointer or yardstick that can be held as a straight "line" that "goes" in different directions, boxes, bowls, table tops, and pedestals can all be experimented with as seen from different points of view. The children become alert to observe and remember views of buildings along a street. The seeming convergence of parallels "receding" into the distance and the idea of horizon as eye-level line are explained. Someone in the class has heard of "vanishing points," but the concepts of what is meant by perspective generally are vague and ambiguous until the subject is demonstrated and experimented with by the children themselves. The "to-me-ness" of an individual point of view is the larger general principle that emerges from a study of perspective.

Some color theory and demonstration are presented, but here again the experimental method is preferred so that the children can discover for themselves how so subjective a factor as color can be made to serve their personal purposes rather than be made to follow rules. Various art materials are from time to time made available in addition to the usual drawing media. Experimentation with these is encouraged and introductory instruction is given. Oil paints are found to be workable in ways that water color and tempera are not.

Building up a form in modeling clay is a method different from the cutting away of extraneous material surrounding a form "contained within" a block of soap or wood.

When such matters are being studied, a visit to look at certain works of art in the museum galleries is most profitable. The students may there see for themselves the ways in which expert handling of the particular materials and tools can achieve the desired effects. Materials and methods of using them are put in their proper relation to the work of art as *means* to an end. The human being, the artist, chooses the end. He has available to his purpose a variety of modes and material means for expression of his idea and feeling.

Definite solutions to problems of practice such as the rendering of light can also be illustrated by similar direct and specific reference to the work of masters, after an elementary classroom explanation of how our seeing is conditioned by light.

Continually, respect for the tools and materials of one's craft must be taught, because children are not by nature careful, and yet they desire to become responsible and competent. The good craftsman and his concern for quality in all his workmanship are ideals appropriately upheld before this age group that is accustomed to having its activities regarded as inconsequential play.

Although the direction of such a course is, on the surface, objective and somewhat technical with a view to satisfying the practical and intellectual curiosity of the youngsters, there is scope for much variety and some stimulation of aesthetic interest. The students are kept interested in coming regularly because they seldom know in advance what the next lesson will be. If it was something they "hated" or "never could do" the last time it was presented, perhaps this time they will find it more within their powers. Or there may be a recurring session of a kind that was especially enjoyable to some among them—a landscape assignment in the Japanese Tea Garden, perhaps (pictures 47 and 49)—and that they are especially eager to try again. Within the repertory there are frequent returns to the same kind of lesson during the term without actual repetition. Occasionally, on field trip days, choice of destination is made by majority vote at the beginning of the period.

Children's development is not steady and regularly paced but discontinuous, with much overlapping of stages. Rapid strides forward alternate with a certain amount of backtracking and periods of standing still. This process varies, moreover, from individual to individual,[13] and so planning of class work must allow for such differences.

47

48

Every few weeks a session is held in which no assignment is made but everyone has "free choice." Each student may choose either to use the assortment of materials in the classroom or to go with one or two others to draw from a motif in one of the several familiar locations the class has worked in previously. Children who would find drawing and painting from memory or imagination a boring prospect if it were the usual routine often welcome the opportunity on these days. The teacher makes the rounds of galleries, garden, and natural history museum as well as the classroom, to offer help if it is needed. Each of the little groups has the responsibility of working independently of adult supervision during the absences of the teacher. Their previous work on assigned lessons has helped them focus attention and concentrate on a selected subject, so "free choice" does not result in aimless doodling.

Perhaps one should not call any of this education in art, for it is no more than teaching the use of pencil, charcoal, crayon, or brush to mark down what one can see and understand about the things one looks at. It is primarily a series of exercises in observing and visualizing. One need not minimize, however, the arduousness of a task requiring intense concentration and effort; it is as hard as learning to read and to write concurrently. The additional complexities of aesthetic composition, of appreciating and interpreting the beauty in what one sees or does, would be too much to expect, certainly too much to require of pupils at this stage. At best, the teacher can call attention to distinctive qualities and be enthusiastic about specific instances when they do appear in a student's work. Here, too, the sense of the whole, the feeling for unique

49

and expressive character are gradually acquired. Meaningful synthesis can only follow earnest analysis for beginners whose approach seems naturally additive. Most of them have never yet seen the forest for the trees.

These children tend to be very critical of their accomplishments from a realistic representational point of view, but every one of them does learn sooner or later to accept the idea that no picture can ever be identical with the reality it may represent—a prevalent and delusive hope or wish that should be put aside with other childish things at a proper time, in order that something better may take its place. They discover also that every picture is subject to the artist's own intention, his mind and will and personal feeling, which are aspects of his individuality and not a communally shared "truth" in any objective sense. The acceptance of a work of art as the artist's *created symbol* for what he can see and think and feel and not as an attempt to counterfeit a public physical fact is the fundamental lesson to be learned by these students before they will ever become ready to produce art of their own or appreciate the art of others.

As for the formation of a personal taste and style and a positive appreciation of aesthetic quality in a work of art, the prosaic materialism and fascination with facts are often too dominant to permit much growth at this time. There are occasional exceptions to literal-mindedness among the nine-to-eleven-year-olds; as they grow into puberty the children do awaken to new perceptions they were not capable of before and they may develop new susceptibilities and new responsiveness to aesthetic appeal.[14]

Meanwhile, testing, challenging, dogmatizing on the part of children are the measuring of themselves against contemporaries and adults. They ask thus indirectly for certainties about themselves and the world they and we live in together. What William James called "the native absolutism of the human mind" operates over and over again to block a view of the world large enough to include more than one opinion. It is a major obstacle to be overcome at this stage if development and learning are to continue into adulthood.[15] Children want not to be deluded. They seem to want very much to be guaranteed the "correctness" of any knowledge, belief, or opinion that they adopt for their own. As relativism is alien to their inclination, they struggle to simplify complex and conflicting ideas in order to accept or to reject, not merely to consider and compare or to contemplate possibilities. What is often sought by minds at this stage of maturing (*regardless of age*) is an authoritarian resolution of their doubts by some firm dogmatist who acts as if he knows all the answers and can vouch for their absolute truth.

This is a stage of growth that needs, as do all others, to be accommodated and then passed beyond to what properly comes next. Children do need to be shown in all honesty, to have it proved to them through their own experience, that no simple set of rules, no single arbitrary system is great enough to encompass all of

52

HAND OF A
BUDDHA

what human beings are capable of achieving. The ways of art as of life are as many and as diverse as human personality, even though every particular society rules out some possible choices. Our own is regarded as free because it does offer a relatively extensive range of opportunity for each person to discover and follow a way that can be truly his own and not merely an imposed pattern to which he is required to conform as in primitive tribal or doctrinaire totalitarian societies.[16]

Art demonstrates the truth of diversity and multiple possibility open to the inquiring human spirit. In learning this, children learn that they may become, as their experience widens and deepens, more adult in their appreciations, more at ease with themselves and with others, less subject to the delusions and frustrations of childhood. At every stage of their development children depend on adults to help them out of the limiting conditions of childhood.

Teachers and parents who regard their relation to children as essentially that of older guides and friends to individuals eager to pursue the human adventure do not try to prescribe or determine what that adventure shall be. Some of the children may indeed become artists. All of them may derive from their study of art an alert and competent skill in perception and facility in visualizing. They may also learn to feel more friendly toward ways that are not their own and so become less primitively hostile in their approach to the new and unfamiliar. So equipped they will be able to participate more fully in whatever share of the human adventure becomes theirs.

he moved!

3. Expression and appreciation (ages 12–15)

When children of twelve or older come to the museum for art instruction they are invited to become members of a group called the Art Club. Whether or not they have previously attended the museum classes for younger children, it is assumed that their interest in art, serious enough to lead them into this independent search for instruction, is also of a sort that can profit especially from individual attention and guidance. The Art Club (which has no officers, committees, dues, or other organizational features) offers, therefore, something of a compromise between class instruction and private lessons for these older students. It meets at least once a week after school in the classroom for discussion and work.

The students are expected to provide their own materials if they can, but drawing materials are available for all. Each one works on his own individually chosen project, either in the classroom or nearby so that the teacher will be conveniently on hand for consultation and advice as needed. Painting in oil or water color, clay modeling, pastel and charcoal drawing are the choices open to the students. Commercial techniques for cartooning or fashion illustration and the use of short-cut trick equipment (numbers painting kits, "Dresden" ware decorating, etc.) are not included as acceptable activities for these occasions because the instruction offered has to do with aesthetic values to be discovered and experienced in the fine arts. Hobby and craft groups exist elsewhere.

The teacher offers suggestions for practice and points out problems to be worked on independently by various students according to their needs and abilities. Sometimes, these boys and girls have had no previous art instruction but have patiently achieved what they know through earnest trial-and-error experimentation. Thus, it often happens that some of the assignments of the intermediate course are equally well suited to Art Club members. (Pictures 53, 54, and 55.)

Along with instructing in art techniques and practices, the teacher of children this age can awaken in them a real appreciation for authentic works of art, especially if the class is held in a museum or art center where original examples are exhibited. Here it is possible to encourage responsiveness to a wider variety of art than has previously been known to the student.[17] To practice an art means to become interested in learning what other artists have done, and so the whole field of history of art, of ideas, of civilization, may become an exciting and vivid experience. Vicarious participation replaces the dull study of impersonal facts about the past.

The living work of art expresses the thought and feeling of the individual human being whose actual life and creative work were accomplished within a milieu—a time and place and way of life that the artist shared with the people of his community. The sense of being linked with all of humanity through the expressive symbols that we use for communication profoundly stimulates our spiritual development. Such illumination brings about an effective integration of intellect and sensibility which education might ideally be expected to achieve. When an art museum provides its community with opportunity for this kind of experience it serves a fundamental cultural purpose; for this reason classes in creative art as means for developing aesthetic appreciation are appropriately held in places where great works are on exhibition.

The Art Club children are capable of much self-direction—more, indeed, than their usual home and school routines permit them. In creative activity this ability is fundamental, for nothing original or truly expressive of the individual can be done by persons dependent on others for their motivations and ideas. For the most part these students are eager to learn, in the sense that learning means initiative and a positive chosen action, not a chore imposed from without. Whatever pertains to art is regarded as a subject for classroom discussion, and individual work projects often arise from the challenge of such contributions and exchanges of ideas. Art is regarded as personally developmental, a mode of assimilating and giving form to experience that is significant to the artist.

Once in a while, a young person is brought to be "trained" in drawing and painting. The approach is that of presenting a passive, docile creature to be taught to perform with agility some trick that he might learn to do in response to the word of command. The adult in charge of the youngster is usually very positive, too, as to what the child may (or, more often, may not) do during class time, such as using some materials but not others, or remaining in the classroom itself until called for, even though a visit to the galleries might be what appropriate instruction requires of the student. Dictation to the teacher of exactly what the child is to achieve and the way in which it is to be done is not unheard of. Such situations become even more preposterous when one hears the stale old words about not knowing anything about art beyond the narrow limits of what this particular person happens to like.

What one hopes for in such cases is a restoration of human spirit in a damaged, intimidated child through the stimulating freedom of the weekly art period. Happily, encounters like this become fewer as time goes by and as more and more parents are sympathetic and interested in encouraging their children's wish to study art. One hears less about the evils of time-wasting and the need to start young learning the trade that will eventually make one wealthy. There is more agreement in our time about the important values of art in a happy, well-rounded, good life.

It must also be acknowledged that a teacher is apt to impose personal tastes and prejudices even when such an effect is consciously guarded against. In order to teach at all, a person must have confidence and conviction as to the importance of the subject taught and its value to the student. The teaching-learning situation being an intricately ethical one involving human

trust and human obligation, awareness of being subject to human error is the only protection a conscientious teacher can have against becoming dogmatic, but it is often impossible to prevent misevaluation on the part of a student.

It is not possible to describe the art teaching that takes place at this level, nor even to evaluate very accurately its results. Partly, this is so because the relationship between student and teacher is based on a shared enthusiasm pursued with confidence in the worth of achievement. The subject is what teacher and student are both concerned with, and the teacher's additional concern for the individual student's development is balanced by the student's quest for insights that the teacher may be able to suggest. Partly, too, this period of a student's life that might include participation in the museum's program of art education is crowded with other interests and activities.

Pupils go on to many other things that the teacher seldom knows of. At rare intervals over the years word may come back of where Susie is going to college, or of Jim's return from Korea, or of Marilyn's prize at art school, or of Dick's studying now in Mexico. How can one measure objectively the value of this particular adolescent experience among others? All teachers proceed on faith. My belief is that art throughout childhood counts importantly in the human development toward full maturity. These young ones are becoming adults whose minds and sensibilities have been encouraged to grow in just proportion to their physical growth. It seems to me that they may continue capable of growth in these invisible dimensions throughout a lifetime.

A few Art Club members through interest and effort develop their ability and increase their understanding enough during their time of attendance so that they can think visually and express their thought and feeling in visual terms. Then time and experience of life remain still necessary if eventually they are to use this power for the creation of art whose significance may be recognized by others.[18] Whether or not they ever do become professional artists is not, after all, so important; it matters more that they become capable of understanding the aesthetic expressions of others through their own personal experience of creating.

Meanwhile, the longed-for recognition of progressive achievement comes—for one or another or several of these earnest learners—when they are welcomed into the adults' studio-classroom at the museum, where they may participate as equals with grownups in the making and doing of art. Here they may draw or paint from the model, receive criticism and advice on an adult level, attend the various courses, and engage confidently in what is an acknowledged adult activity— no longer something that can be discounted as just an amusing pastime for children.

NOTES

NOTES

[1] "The symbol-making function is one of man's primary activities, like eating, looking, or moving about. It is the fundamental process of his mind, and goes on all the time. Sometimes we are aware of it, sometimes we merely find its results, and realize that certain experiences have passed through our brains and have been digested there. . . . For if the material of thought is symbolism, then the thinking organism must be forever furnishing symbolic versions of its experiences, in order to let thinking proceed. As a matter of fact, it is not the essential act of thought that is symbolization, but an act *essential to thought,* and prior to it. Symbolization is the essential act of mind; and mind takes in more than what is commonly called thought. Only certain products of the symbol-making brain can be used according to the canons of discursive reasoning. . . . The material furnished by the senses is constantly wrought into *symbols,* which are our elementary ideas. Some of these ideas can be combined and manipulated in the manner we call 'reasoning.' Others do not lend themselves to this use, but are naturally telescoped into dreams, or vapor off in conscious fantasy. . . ." Susanne K. Langer, *Philosophy in a New Key* (New York: Penguin Books, Inc., 1948), pp. 32–33.

[2] ". . . What art expresses is *not* actual feeling, but ideas of feeling; as language does not express actual things and events but ideas of them. Art is expressive through and through—every line, every sound, every gesture; and therefore it is a hundred per cent symbolic." Susanne K. Langer, *Feeling and Form* (New York: Charles Scribner's Sons, 1953), p. 59.

[3] "Nevertheless the sign as such, conventional (arbitrary) and ready-made is not an adequate medium of expression for the young child's thought; he is not satisfied with speaking, he must needs 'play out' what he thinks and symbolize his ideas by means of gestures or objects, and represent things by imitation, drawing, and construction." Jean Piaget, *The Psychology of Intelligence* (New York: Harcourt, Brace & Co., 1950), p. 159.

[4] "The symbol is essentially the expression of the child's present reality." Jean Piaget, *Play, Dreams and Imitation in Childhood* (New York: W. W. Norton & Co., 1951), p. 155.

[5] "There is, however, a certain sense of confusion present in the work of each child. There is a rapid passage of thought from one subject to another, a swift transition, often difficult for a more mature mind to follow. The field of the relevant is wider than that to which we as adults are used in our thinking, and

there is consequently for us an impression of incoherence, a lack of smoothness, an irritating sense of incompleteness. These characteristics are due partly to the child's faulty use of a highly socialized medium of expression, that of language, and partly to the inherent nature of childish thought, and to its essential difference, albeit a matter of degree, from that of adult thought. Also, the child's tendency to ego-centrism makes it difficult for him to realize how little of his subjective meaning is conveyed to others by his speech." Ruth Griffiths, *A Study of Imagination in Early Childhood* (London: Kegan Paul, 1935), p. 115.

[6] "The concept [word] is general and communicable, the image is singular and egocentric." Jean Piaget, *Play, Dreams and Imitation in Childhood* (New York: W. W. Norton & Co., 1951), p. 223.

[7] "The natural attention span of four-years-old children has been shown to be from five to ten minutes at one occupation; and of this time approximately one-third is spent in moods of distraction or day-dreaming; from two to three minutes only does it seem natural at this age for continuous attention to be directed upon a task. . . . The average child of five years is unable to sustain the conditon of concentrated attention for more than a very few minutes, and even during those few minutes he is liable to drift from the problem in hand to the less strenuous work of phantasy. It is this type of thought to which he so readily turns, and which indeed seems to be his characteristic mode of thinking, that it is intended to describe under the title of imagination. . . . This type of thought has been described as 'undirected'. . . . To understand the day-dream is to understand the child." Ruth Griffiths, *A Study of Imagination in Early Childhood* (London: Kegan Paul, 1935), pp. 10–12.

[8] "If we consider children's drawing as expression of a natural process of learning, we find that its chief characteristics can be described as imitation and self-expression, repetition and new acquisitions." Helga Eng, *The Psychology of Children's Drawings* (London: Kegan Paul, 1931), p. 184. Piaget develops a theory of learning based on the processes of *assimilation* of new knowledge or experience to old and the *accommodation* of old to include new. William James used a rather poetic figure to describe learning as being woven with the weft of invention on the warp of imitation.

[9] A little girl of seven drew a picture of a house, cut along one side and the top of the door so that she could fold it open. Then she turned the paper over and drew the people "inside"

the house, in their rooms on the reverse of the facade. It disturbed her momentarily that these people could not be seen through the front windows of her first drawing even if she were to cut openings, a procedure she realized would destroy her picture of the interior. She resolved the dilemma by drawing some faces of the family in the facade windows and did not feel that any new problem had been created that would require her to account for these appearances by additional or revised drawing of the interior view on the other side of the paper. (No windows had been indicated in her peopled rooms.)

[10] Either conventional perspective or "bird's-eye" views would solve the dilemma here, but such schemes are not, in my experience, generally available to the children's thinking until they are about nine, and then they have to be presented as direct instruction. In the scientifically oriented English school conducted by Susan Isaacs for selected pupils, younger children were able to discover such principles for themselves as a result of certain experiments. They made a model of the school and garden in clay, climbed ladders in order to look down from above, and figured out that what an airplane pilot would see of them and their surroundings would be only the tops of things: their heads, treetops but not trunks, roofs but not walls. This led to a project of map-making to indicate locations of familiar places near the children's school. The map was put to use—tested—as a guide for reaching a nearby village. I do not know in what way these children's other drawings may have been affected by their new knowledge.

A less sophisticated logic is illustrated by the question of the four-year-old child (American) who always went to watch the airplane take off from the airport when his grandmother's visit was over. He enjoyed the experience and liked to watch until the plane was out of sight. When he himself was to embark on his first trip in an airplane he was alarmed and reluctant rather than delighted at the prospect, and after the passengers had settled themselves and the plane was speeding down the runway he asked his companion, "When do we start to get littler?"

[11] ". . . The important part in art activities is the influence which the creative process has on our children and not the final product. How far contests and competitions do justice to this all-important contribution of art to the child's growth needs thorough discussion. . . . Instead of being proud when one's own child is the happy winner of a prize, while many others are the remaining frustrated ones, parents should awaken to the harmful and devastating influence which art contests have on the

personalities of their children." Viktor Lowenfeld, *Your Child and His Art* (New York: The Macmillan Co., 1954), p. 49–51.

[12] "More than anything else in experience, the arts mold our actual life of feeling. . . .

"Artistic training is, therefore, the education of feeling, as our usual schooling in factual subjects, and logical skills such as mathematical 'figuring' or simple argumentation (principles are hardly ever explained), is the education of thought. Few people realize that the real education of emotion is not the 'conditioning' effected by social approval and disapproval, but the tacit, personal, illuminating contact with symbols of feeling. Art education, therefore, is neglected, left to chance, or regarded as a cultural veneer." Susanne K. Langer, *Feeling and Form* (New York: Charles Scribner's Sons, 1953), p. 401.

[13] "It must be remembered that the mind does not grow on a straight and even front. The course of development is uneven (in some children more so than others)." Arnold Gesell and Frances L. Ilg, *The Child from Five to Ten* (New York: Harper & Bros., 1946), p. 26.

[14] "Generally speaking, the activity of self-expression cannot be taught. Any application of an external standard, whether of technique or of form, immediately induces inhibitions, and frustrates the whole aim. The role of the teacher is that of attendant, guide, inspirer, psychic midwife.

"Observation is almost entirely an acquired skill. . . . In most cases the eye (and the other organs of sensation) have to be trained, both in observation (directed perception) and in notation. . . .

"As for appreciation, this can undoubtedly be developed by teaching, but as we have seen, appreciation is just as relative to psychological type as is expression, but in so far as by appreciation we mean a response to other people's modes of expression, then the faculty is only likely to develop as one aspect of social adaptation, and cannot be expected to show itself much before the age of adolescence." Herbert Read, *Education Through Art* (London: Faber & Faber, Ltd., 1944), p. 206.

[15] "The natural attitude of the mind is belief, and doubt or hypothesis are complex, derived behaviours whose development can be traced between the ages of seven and eleven up to the level of formal operations, at which there is a real distinction between thought and spontaneous acceptance." Jean Piaget, *Play, Dreams and Imitation in Childhood* (New York: W. W. Norton & Co., 1951), p. 167.

[16] Ruth Benedict, *Patterns of Culture* (New York: New American Library, 1946), pp. 21, 219.

[17] "The entire qualification one must have for understanding art is responsiveness. That is primarily a natural gift, related to creative talent, yet not the same thing; like talent, where it exists in any measure it may be heightened by experience or reduced by adverse agencies. Since it is intuitive, it cannot be taught; but the free exercise of artistic intuition often depends on clearing the mind of intellectual prejudices and false conceptions that inhibit people's natural responsiveness." Susanne K. Langer, *Feeling and Form* (New York: Charles Scribner's Sons, 1953), p. 396.

[18] "Essentially it is a difference in maturation. . . . In so far as technical skill is the ability adequately to express a mental perception, or a feeling, it will contribute to the aesthetic value of the act of expression. . . . The very process of maturation seems to adjust skill to the requirements of the child at any particular stage of development. The skill is developed by the drawing, not the drawing by the skill." Herbert Read, *Education Through Art* (London: Faber & Faber, Ltd., 1944), p. 208.

READING LIST